STANFORD

Three Intermezzi

Op. 13

for clarinet and piano

Edited by

Colin Bradbury

CHESTER MUSIC

EDITOR'S NOTE

Two works for the clarinet by Charles Villiers Stanford (1852-1924) are well known; the **Concerto Op. 80** of 1902, and the **Sonata Op. 129** of 1918. By the time he wrote the first of these, Stanford was an established composer with over seventy works to his credit. He was Professor of Music at Cambridge University, Professor of Composition at the Royal College of Music, and had honorary degrees as Doctor of Music from both Cambridge and Oxford. In 1901 he had received a knighthood.

The **Three Intermezzi Op. 13**, however, were composed before he was thirty, whilst he was still organist at Trinity College, Cambridge. He wrote them for Francis Galpin, an undergraduate who was later to become well known as the distinguished scholar and collector, Canon Galpin, after whom the society devoted to old musical instruments is named. The first performance was given by Galpin and Stanford at a Wednesday Popular Concert of the Cambridge University Musical Society on February 18th, 1880.

Much has been made of the influence of Brahms on Stanford's music, and Stanford was obviously familiar with the Brahms **Clarinet Trio**, the **Quintet** and the two **Sonatas Op. 120** when he wrote his own **Concerto** and **Sonata**. No such models, however, influenced his masterly use of the clarinet in the **Intermezzi**. They were written eleven years before Brahms composed his first great clarinet work, the **Trio Op. 114**, and fifteen years before Stanford could possibly have heard the Brahms Sonatas.

Apart from the correction of obvious printer's errors and some notational changes to conform to modern practice, this edition follows the original Novello edition of 1880.

Colin Bradbury

Three Intermezzi have been recorded by
Colin Bradbury and Oliver Davies on
Discourses ABM 29

THREE INTERMEZZI

Charles Villiers Stanford
Op. 13
Edited by Colin Bradbury

No. I

25
31
cresc.
mf
37
dim.
43
Allegretto leggiero (♩ =76)
p
mp
simile

48
f
p
p staccato
f
54
f
p
f
p
59
f
f
64
f
f
p

69
dim.
p
rall.
dim.
pp
ppp
rall.
75
Tempo I
mf
p
legato
mf
con Ped.
80
cresc.
85
cresc.
dim.
con 8va

91
97
con 8va
con 8va
103
di - mi - nu - en -
109
- do
pp
pp
Ped.

No. II

Allegro agitato (♩. =144)
Clarinet in B♭
Piano
mp
mp
cresc.
cresc.
6
p
p
12
cresc.
cresc.
18
f
p
f
p
f
p
f
p
f
non legato

24
f
30
sf
sf
cresc.
f
36
f
sf
42
sf
sf
dim.
sf

48
p
pp
54
Tranquillo (♩ = ♩.)
pp
63
72
cresc.
p

79
p
cresc.
p
86
pp
mf
pp
94
p
103
cresc.
mp

111
cresc.
117
f
f
non
legato
123
f
129
tr

136
sf
dim.
dim.
143
sf
sf
dim.
p
dim.
149
pp
pp
pp
156
pp
con 8va

No. III

Allegretto scherzando (♩ =104)
Clarinet in B♭
Piano
mp
p
p
5
cresc.
f
il basso sempre staccato
tr
f
9
p
p
tr
tr
13
p
cresc.
cresc.

mf
mf
cresc.
f
f
sf
largamente
ten.
p
pp
mp
con Ped.
cantabile
legato
pp
mp

36
pp
cresc.
mf
f
pesante
f
con 8va
41
cresc.
fp
46
sfp
cresc.
50
f
f
p

54
3
p
58
cresc.
cresc.
f
5
63
cresc.
cresc.
6
ff
ff
tr
3
67
p
dim.
p
f
rit.
f
rit.

SELECTED MUSIC FOR CLARINET AND PIANO

Flute	Editor: Trevor Wye	Clarinet	Editor: Thea King
Oboe	Editor: James Brown	Bassoon	Editor: William Waterhouse

Saxophone Editor: Paul Harvey

A growing collection of volumes from Chester Music, containing a wide range of pieces from different periods.

CLARINET SOLOS VOLUME I

Bizet	Entr'acte from Carmen
Labor	Allegretto from Quintet for Clarinet, Strings and Piano
Lefèvre	Allegro from Sonata No. 3
Mozart	Minuet from Serenade for Wind Octet K. 375
Mozart	Il Mio Tesoro
Schubert	Trio from the Minuet of Octet, Op. 166
Schubert	Allegretto from Symphony No. 3
Tchaikovsky	Allegro Con Grazia from Symphony No. 6

CLARINET SOLOS VOLUME II

Beethoven	Allegro (Finale) from Wind Sextet Op. 71
Crusell	Minuet from Quartet in C minor Op. 4
Crusell	Andante Moderato from Concerto in B♭ Op. 1
Glazounov	Allegretto from the ballet The Seasons
Mendelssohn	Andante from Konzertstück in D minor Op. 114
Molter	Moderato from Concerto in D
Rimsky-Korsakov	Andante from Concerto for Clarinet and Military Band
Weber	From Introduction, Theme and Variations

Also available:
CLARINET DUETS VOLUMES I, II & III
Further details on request

CHESTER MUSIC